Places We Live

Living Beside a
River

Ellen Labrecque

Heinemann
raintree

© 2015 Heinemann Raintree
an imprint of Capstone Global Library, LLC
Chicago, Illinois

To contact Capstone Global Library, please call 800-747-4992, or visit our web site www.capstonepub.com

Edited by James Benefield and Brenda Haugen
Designed by Richard Parker
Original illustrations © Capstone Global Library 2015
Picture research by Jo Miller
Production by Helen McCreath
Originated by Capstone Global Library Ltd

Library of Congress Cataloging-in-Publication Data
Labrecque, Ellen.
  Living beside a river / Ellen Labrecque.
      pages cm.—(Places we live)
  Includes bibliographical references and index.
  ISBN 978-1-4846-0801-2 (hb)—ISBN 978-1-4846-0808-1 (pb)—ISBN 978-1-4846-0822-7 (ebook) 1. Rivers—Juvenile literature. 2. Stream ecology—Juvenile literature. 3. Human geography—Juvenile literature. I. Title.

  GF63.L33 2015
  304.20916'93—dc23   2014013627

This book has been officially leveled by using the F&P Text Level Gradient™ Leveling System.

Acknowledgments
We would like to thank the following for permission to reproduce photographs: Alamy: Paul Springett C, 25; AP Images: Kusumadireza, 26; Corbis: Tiziana and Gianni Baldizzone, 5; Getty Images: National Geographic/Timothy G. Laman, 19, The Image Bank/Zigy Kaluzny-Charles Thatcher, 21; Newscom: Andre Jenny Stock Connection Worldwide, 14, Danita Delimont Photography/David Wall, 4, Danita Delimont Photography/Pete Oxford, 13, imago stock & people, 27; Shutterstock: Alexander A. Trofimov, 20, alice-photo, 12, Dan Schreiber, 10, dimbar76, cover, Dobresum, 9, EpicStockMedia, 24, Frontpage, 6, Grisha Bruev, 18, Lisa-Lisa, 16, Lukasz Janyst, 11, maigi, 15, Neale Cousland, 22, Peter Stuckings, 8, Ritu Manoj Jethani, 17, Strahil Dimitrov, 23.

Design Elements: Shutterstock: donatas1205, Olympus.

We would like to thank Rachel Bowles for her invaluable help in the preparation of this book.

Printed in the United States of America.
042019   001965

Contents

Some words are shown in bold, **like this**. You can find out what they mean by looking in the glossary.

What Is a River?

Rivers are natural streams of running water. They can start as **springs**, lakes, and **glaciers**. Rivers make **channels** and flow into other lakes or rivers. They end in a mouth, which flows into the sea, often through an **estuary** or a **delta**.

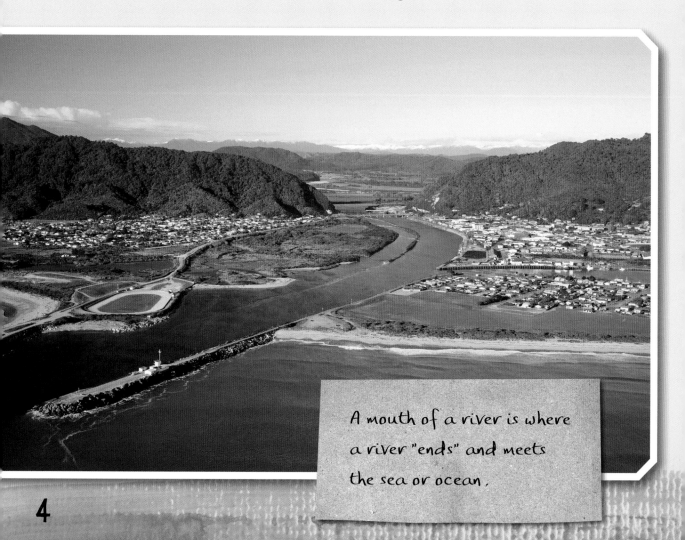

A mouth of a river is where a river "ends" and meets the sea or ocean.

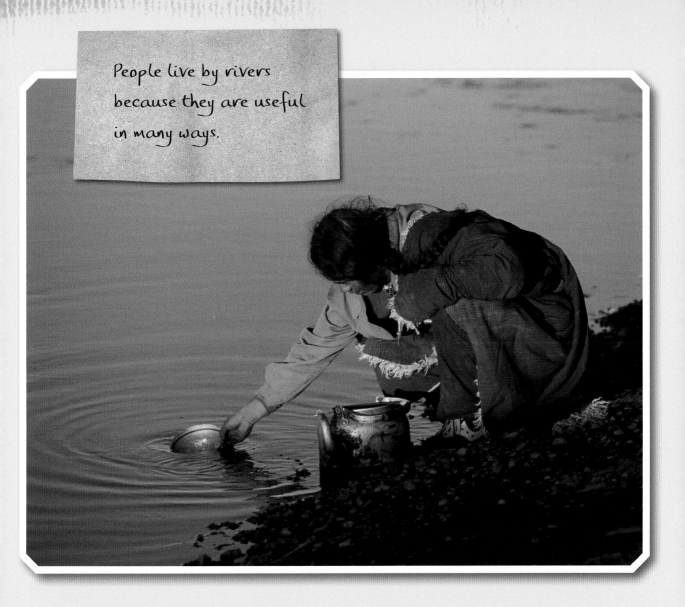

People live by rivers because they are useful in many ways.

Animals, plants, and people cannot live without water, so rivers can be great places to live! Living by a river means you can easily travel, move things around, fish, and farm.

Where Are Rivers?

Rivers are found on every **continent** and on all types of land. They begin on mountains or hills. Here, rainwater or water from melted snow collects and forms streams. As the stream collects more water, it forms a river.

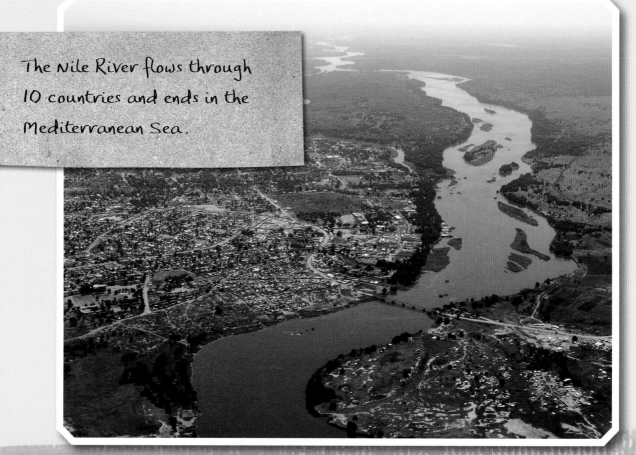

The Nile River flows through 10 countries and ends in the Mediterranean Sea.

Earth's longest rivers

1. Nile River, Africa: 4,132 miles (6,650 kilometers)

2. Amazon River, South America: 3,976 miles (6,400 kilometers)

3. Yangtze River, China: 3,915 miles (6,300 kilometers)

4. Mississippi–Missouri river system, United States: 3,902 miles (6,275 kilometers)

The Nile River has several **sources** that mostly flow into Lake Victoria. On the north end of Lake Victoria, water pours over a waterfall. This is Ripon Falls. It pours into a narrow opening, and this is where the Nile really begins.

Rivers of the Past

Rivers have helped shape our land over thousands of years. Scientists think the Colorado River, in Arizona, eroded the rock to make the Grand Canyon.

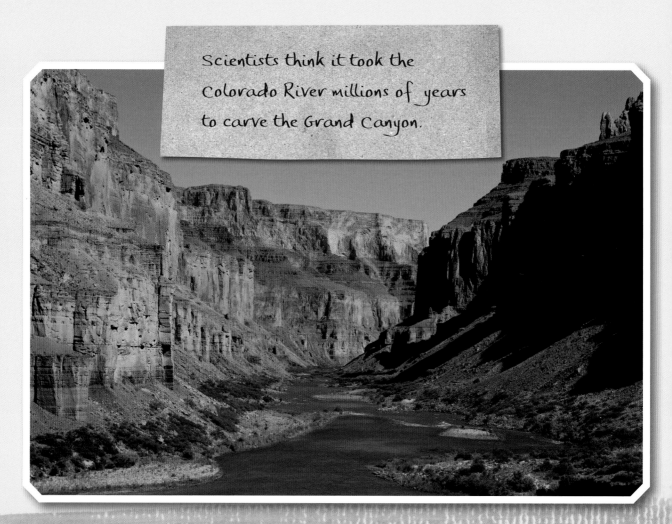

Scientists think it took the Colorado River millions of years to carve the Grand Canyon.

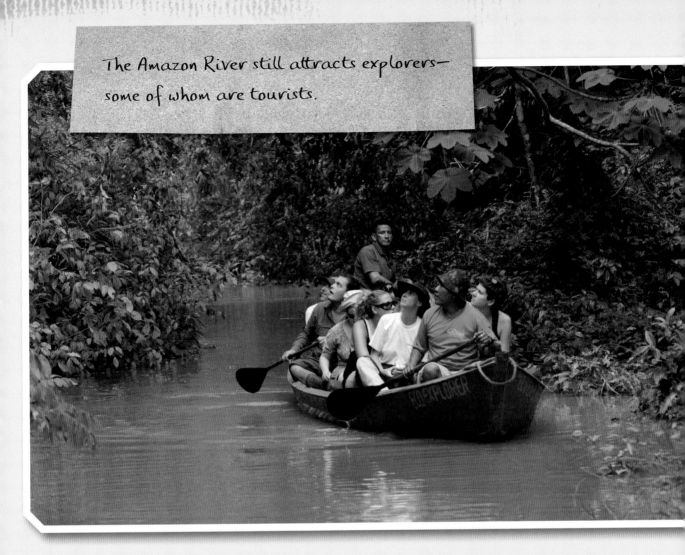

The Amazon River still attracts explorers— some of whom are tourists.

People in the past have followed river paths to explore new parts of the world. Explorers sailed down rivers to discover new parts of Africa and North and South America. There are now cities in some of these places.

Living Beside a River

One of the main reasons people live in **settlements** by a river is food. Rivers create perfect land beside them for growing **crops**. The river also gives farmers water for watering their plants.

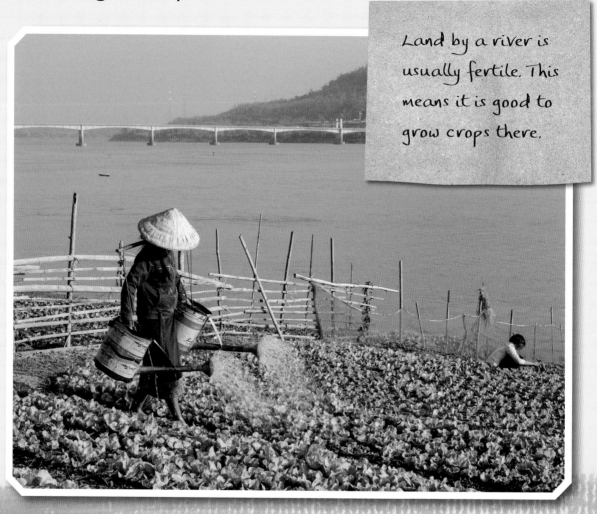

Land by a river is usually fertile. This means it is good to grow crops there.

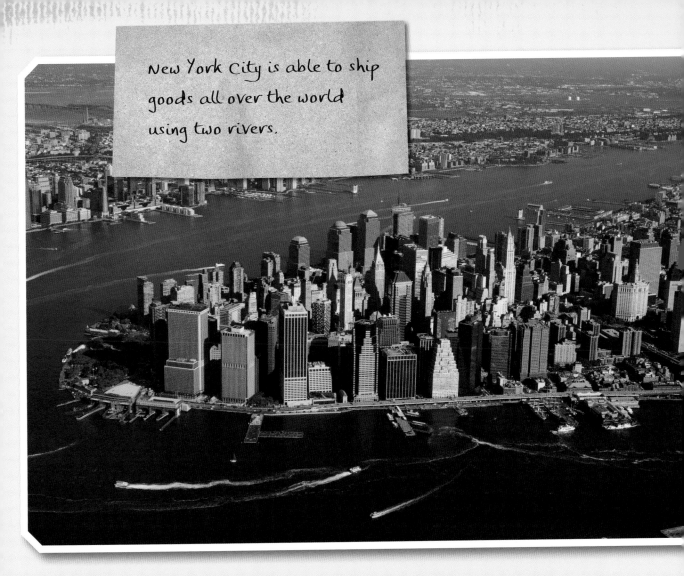

New York City is able to ship goods all over the world using two rivers.

People live by rivers in villages, towns, and cities. Some people even live in floating homes. The biggest city in the United States, New York City, has the Hudson River on one side and the East River on the other.

All Kinds of People

Cities grow around rivers because of **trade**. This started when people bought and sold things such as spices, tea, and sugar. People could travel down rivers and trade from country to country. Trade still happens today.

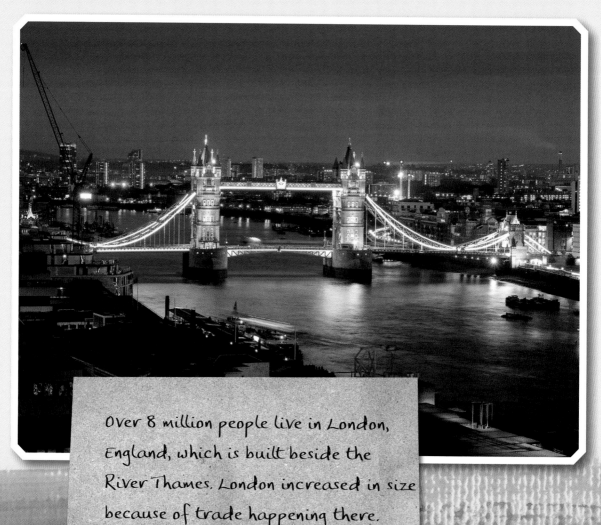

Over 8 million people live in London, England, which is built beside the River Thames. London increased in size because of trade happening there.

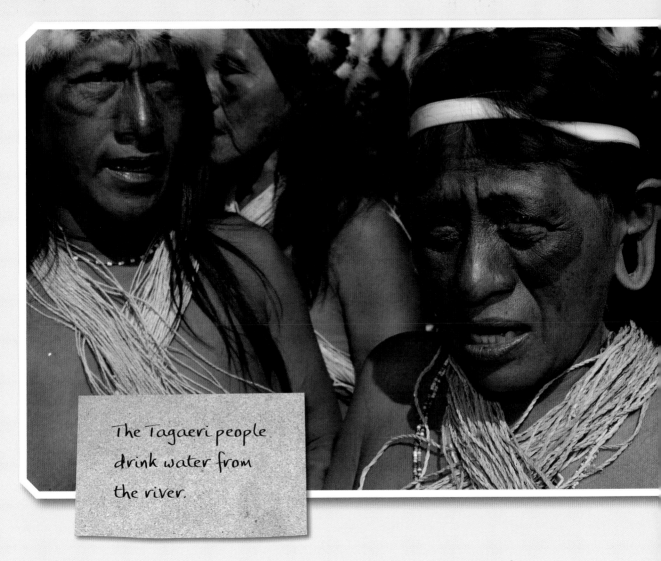

The Tagaeri people drink water from the river.

There are not many cities or towns along the Amazon River in South America. There are mostly rain forests. The Tagaeri people live here as nomads. They don't stay in one place, but instead travel to find food.

Flooding Rivers

The biggest problem with living beside a river is the danger of flooding. Rivers flood when they get too much water from rainfall or melting snow. This makes the water level rise over the **riverbanks**.

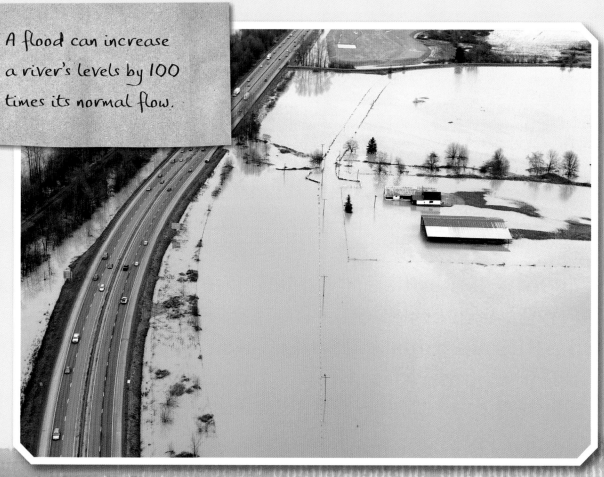

A flood can increase a river's levels by 100 times its normal flow.

Some houses along rivers are built on stilts to keep them dry.

Overflowing river water can destroy anything in its path. It can also drown people. Walls and barriers called floodwalls are built around rivers to stop floods. The Mississippi River in the United States has raised banks called levees.

Canal Living

Rivers are so useful that we have built our own! Canals are dug-out **trenches** that are filled with water. They are made so boats can move things from the sea to places inland.

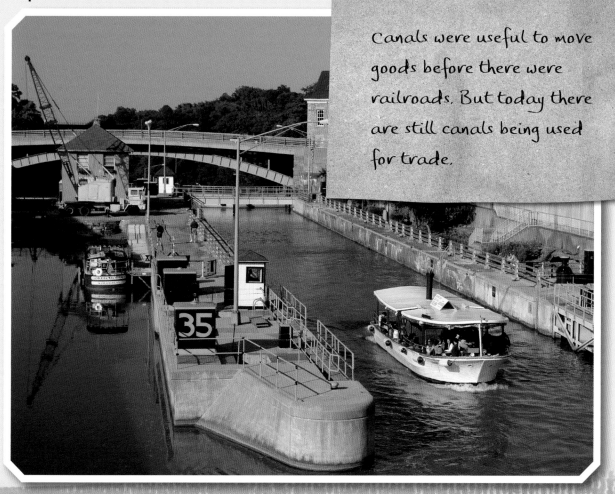

Canals were useful to move goods before there were railroads. But today there are still canals being used for trade.

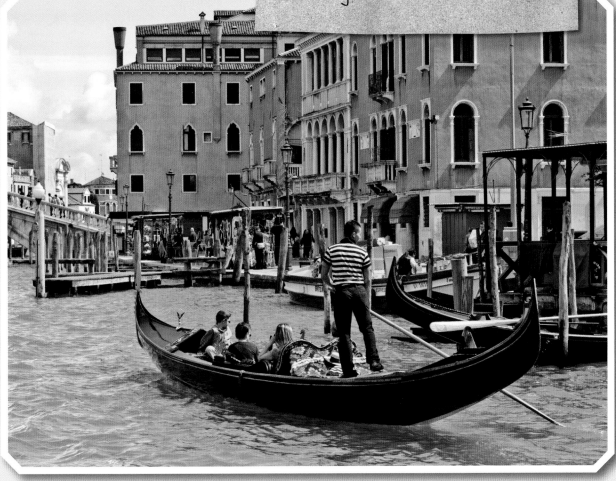

You can only get around Venice on foot or on boats, such as these gondolas.

Venice, Italy, is famous for its canals. It is one of the only cities in the world that has almost no cars. Over 100 canals go through the city and empty into the Adriatic Sea.

Getting Around

People use rivers to move from one place to another. If the river is wide enough, you can sail giant ships down rivers. Some people paddle on rivers in canoes, kayaks, or small rafts.

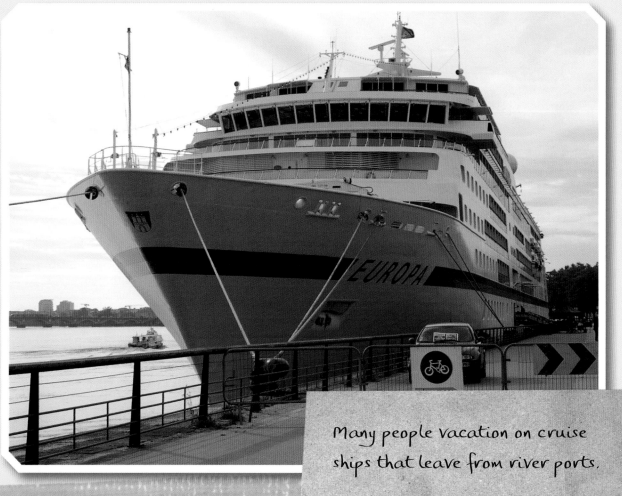

Many people vacation on cruise ships that leave from river ports.

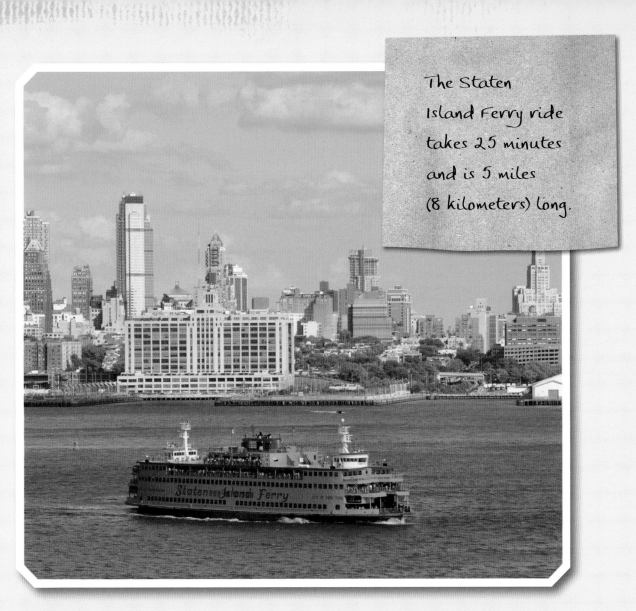

The Staten Island Ferry ride takes 25 minutes and is 5 miles (8 kilometers) long.

Some people use river ferries to travel to work. In the East River, near New York City, the Staten Island Ferry takes 60,000 passengers a day between Staten Island and the city.

Riverbank and Plant Life

We eat a lot of the plant and animal life that lives in and near rivers. For example, rivers are great places to catch fish. Many plants, such as reeds and cattails, grow in the soil by rivers.

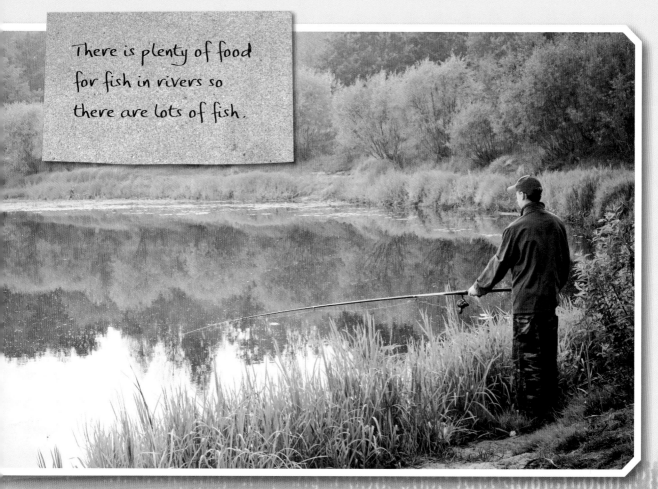

There is plenty of food for fish in rivers so there are lots of fish.

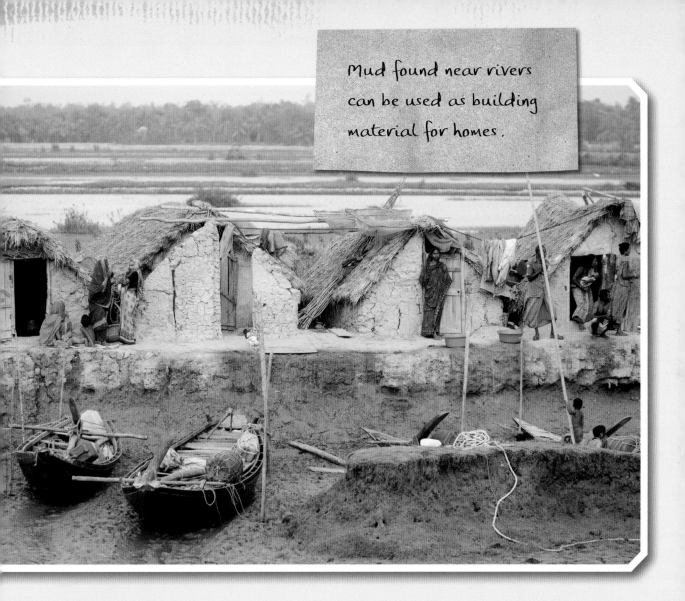

Mud found near rivers can be used as building material for homes.

We find materials such as straw, clay, and mud by rivers. We can use these materials for building. Some people collect river rocks to build paths in their backyards!

What Is Work Like?

You can be a teacher, nurse, or writer and live by a river. But living by a river also offers special jobs. For example, rivers can be popular with tourists. Tourists love everything from water sports to seeing the sights.

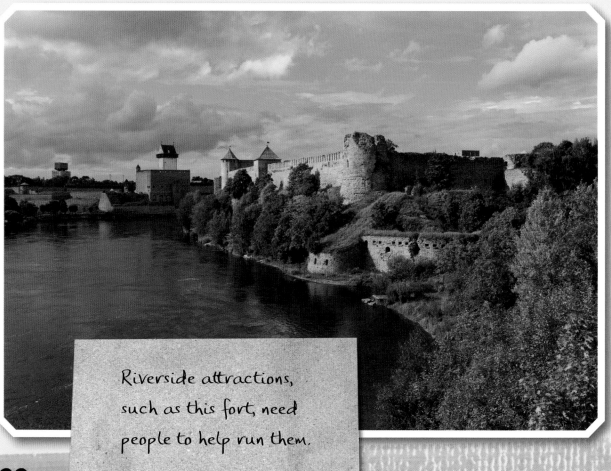

Riverside attractions, such as this fort, need people to help run them.

River engineers can change the direction the water flows in a river.

Some people work by rivers. River engineers study rivers to try to stop flooding and stop **pollution**. Many rivers have large and small shipbuilding yards, providing many different types of jobs.

Fun Things to Do

People visit rivers because they offer many fun things to do. You can swim, fish, and water-ski in rivers. Some of the most popular things to do on a river are kayaking, canoeing, and white water rafting.

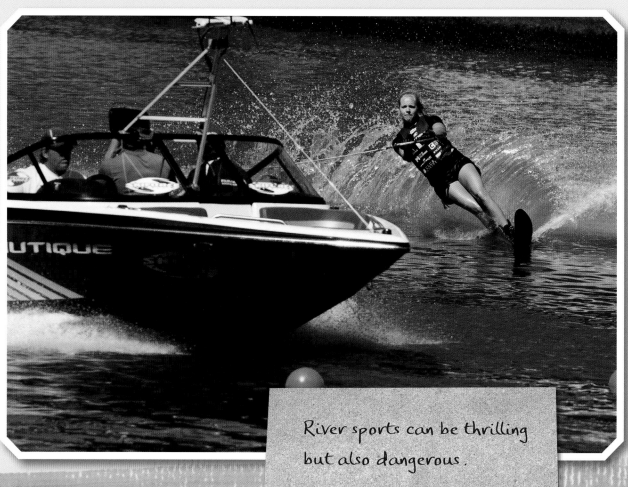

River sports can be thrilling but also dangerous.

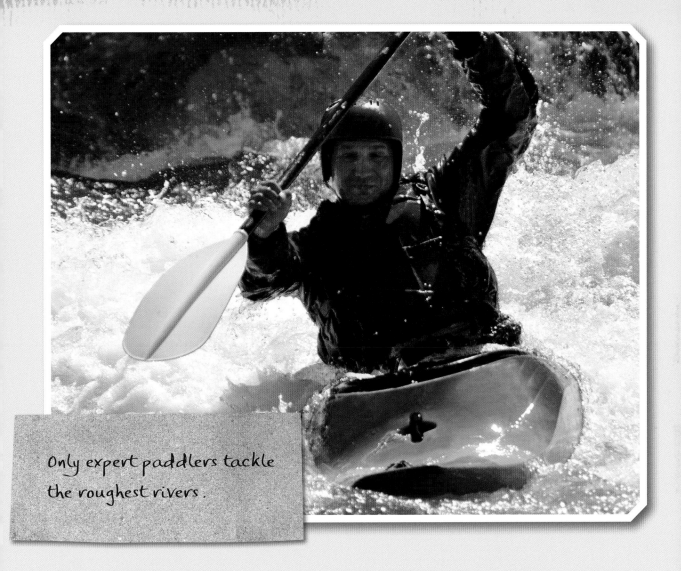

Only expert paddlers tackle the roughest rivers.

Rivers are graded so you can tell how rough the river is. There are six levels or grades. The lowest, Grade 1, means the river is calm and safe. Grade 6 means it is dangerous.

Rivers of the Future

Many rivers today are polluted. The waste comes from cities and factories dumping their trash. Sometimes rivers are **overfished**, too. This leaves people and animals without enough food.

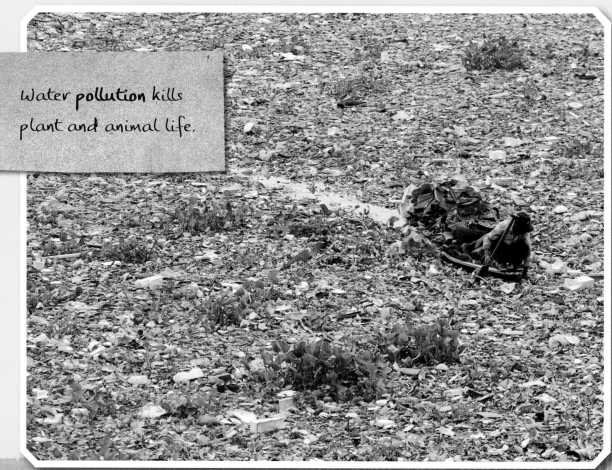

Water **pollution** kills plant and animal life.

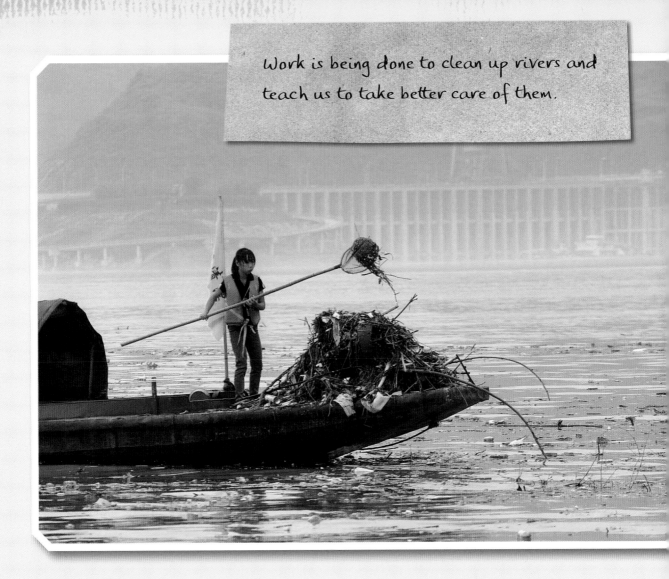

Since 1998, the Living Lands & Water group has picked up over 7 million pounds (15 million kilograms) of river trash. Other groups have planted new trees along **riverbanks**. These can give animals food and places to live.

Fun Facts

- Long ago, people found gold in rivers such as the Klondike River in Canada.

- Races in kayaks and canoes in the summer Olympics can take place on rivers.

- Seventy-six rivers in the world are over 1,000 miles (1,609 kilometers) long.

- The longest single river in the United States is the Missouri River. It is 2,341 miles (3,767 kilometers) long.

- China has a number of the longest rivers in the world running through it. These include the Yangtze River and the Yellow River.

- Most of the world's major cities sit on a river.

Quiz

Which of the following sentences are true? Which are false?

1. Rivers are only found on some continents.

2. Canals are waterways that are human-made.

3. Some people travel to work on rivers.

4. People discovered new places in the world by following rivers.

5. All the rivers around the world are clean.

1. Fals. Rivers are found on all continents.

2. True. Canals are trenches built by people.

3. True. People travel to work on rivers every day.

4. True. Explorers followed rivers to find new places.

5. False. Some rivers are badly polluted. Some people work to clean them up.

Glossary

channel passage through which a river flows

continent any of the world's seven biggest landmasses: Africa, Antarctica, Asia, Australia, Europe, North America, and South America

crop plant grown by people for food

delta triangle-shaped piece of land at the mouth of the river where it flows into an ocean, sea, or lake

eroded when land or rock has been worn or ground down over time by water, ice, snow, or wind

estuary where a river meets the sea; it is salty and has tides

glacier slow-moving icy mass or river of ice

overfish when people have taken too many fish from a river, sea, or lake

pollution garbage, waste, sand, and mud that make the air, land, rivers, or seas dirty and unsafe

riverbank land along a river

settlement place where people live for good, such as a village, town, or city

spring place where rivers can start when underground water reaches the surface

source place where a river starts

trade when you buy and sell things

trench long, narrow ditch. This can be dug by people or it can exist in nature.

Find Out More

Books

Ganeri, Anita. *The World's Most Amazing Rivers* (Landform Top Tens). Chicago: Raintree, 2008.

Parker, Steve. *Pond and River* (DK Eyewitness Books). New York: Dorling Kindersley, 2011.

Waldron, Melanie. *Rivers* (Habitat Survival). Chicago: Raintree, 2013.

Internet sites

Facthound offers a safe, fun way to find Internet sites related to this book. All of the sites on Facthound have been researched by our staff.

Here's all you do:

Visit www.facthound.com

Type in this code: 9781484608012

Index